BORN IN LOCKDOWN

Tolu' A. Akinyemi

First published in Great Britain as a
softback original in 2021

Copyright © Tolu' A. Akinyemi
The moral right of the author has been asserted.
All rights reserved.

No part of this publication may be reproduced, stored in a retrieval system, or transmitted, in any form or by any means, without the prior permission in writing of the author, nor be otherwise circulated in any form of binding or cover other than that in which it is published and without a similar condition including this condition being imposed on the subsequent purchaser.

Cover Design: Buzzdesignz

Published by 'The Roaring Lion Newcastle'
ISBN: 978-1-913636-28-9

Email:
tolu@toluakinyemi.com
author@tolutoludo.com

Website:
www.toluakinyemi.com
www.tolutoludo.com

ALSO BY TOLU' A. AKINYEMI

Dead Lions Don't Roar
(A collection of poetic wisdom for the discerning)

Unravel your Hidden Gems
(A collection of inspirational and motivational essays)

Dead Dogs Don't Bark
(A collection of poetic wisdom for the Discerning Series 2)

Dead Cats Don't Meow
(A collection of poetic wisdom for the Discerning Series 3)

Never Play Games with the Devil
(A collection of poems)

A Booktiful Love
(A collection of poems)

Inferno of Silence
(A collection of short stories)

Black ≠ Inferior
(A collection of poems)

Never Marry a Writer
(A collection of poems)

Everybody Don Kolomental
(A collection of poems)

I am Not a Troublemaker
(Children's Literature)

I Wear Self-Confidence Like a Second Skin
(Children's Literature)

A god in a human body
(A collection of poems)

Dedication

To the frontline workers who gave their all to fight the COVID-19 pandemic. Thank you for your sacrifice and labour of love.

Table of Contents

ACKNOWLEDGEMENTS 1

POEMS 2
PANDEMIC 4
VIRUS.. 5
BOREDOM 6
PALLIATIVES 7
NOT THE END 8
TRAUMA 9
VACCINE WARS... 10
SURVIVORS... 11
ONE GOOD MAN SHORT 12
F*CK – F*CKING 2020 13
F*CK 2020 14
EMPTY ROOMS 15
COVAX 16
ONE JAB 17
GROW SOME BALLS 18
DREAM FAREWELL 19
THE DEAD..20
MASK 21
HOME...22
THIS VIRUS 23
BEWITCHED 24
THUNDERSTORMS...25

CENTURY OLD	26
DREAMS	27
BANKRUPT	28
TOO HOT	29
MY REMEMBRANCE	30
STORIES	31
THE DAYS ARE RUNNING	32
PANDEMIC TIMES	33
FRONTLINE	34
FAKE NEWS	35
BORN IN LOCKDOWN	36
THE GREAT APOCALYPSE	37
FREEDOM DAY	38
COVID SURVIVOR	39
DREAMS	40
FAMILY	42
PASSPORTS	43
DOMESTIC COVID	44
ISOLATION AND LOCKDOWNS	45
EAT THE FUTURE NOW	46
CHILDHOOD	47
STAY HOME, SAVE LIVES	48
BIO	**49**
AUTHOR'S NOTE	52
DEAD LIONS DON'T ROAR	53
DEAD DOGS DON'T BARK	55
DEAD CATS DON'T MEOW	57
UNRAVEL YOUR HIDDEN GEMS	59
NEVER PLAY GAMES WITH THE DEVIL	62
A BOOKTIFUL LOVE	64
INFERNO OF SILENCE	66

BLACK ≠INFERIOR 69
NEVER MARRY A WRITER 72
EVERYBODY DON KOLOMENTAL 74
A GOD IN A HUMAN BODY 76
I AM NOT A TROUBLEMAKER 78
I WEAR SELF-CONFIDENCE LIKE A SECOND SKIN
.... 79

Acknowledgements

Sincere appreciation to God Almighty for the wisdom to write yet another book – I'm indeed grateful and do not take this ability for granted.

A big thank you to my booktiful partner, Olabisi, for always being there to listen to my writings in their raw form and provide invaluable feedback.

To my wonderful children, Isaac and Abigail Akinyemi – Thanks for your support and believing that I am the best poet alive. ☺

Sincere thanks to my wonderful parents, Gabriel and Temidayo Akinyemi – for your endless and immeasurable support in my literary journey.

To my editors, Adeola Gbalajobi and the Hungry Bookstore – Thank you for being a vital part of this booktiful journey.

To everyone who has supported me on my journey to literary acclaim – your support is greatly appreciated.

POEMS

Pandemic

There is a pandemic in my head,

raging like boiling water.

There is a war in my mind,

tugging at the deepest part of my soul.

There is a thunderstorm in my heart,

wreaking havoc like it is doomsday.

Virus

I framed your picture in my heart in hardwood

until COVID crept in

and what remained were broken particles.

Your love in my heart was innocent

and untainted

until COVID crept in

and the veil of deceit was lifted.

The hallmark of our love were red roses,

flowers and *sexting*

until COVID crept in

and it became a virus.

Boredom

The silence in this house is eating me up like termites ravaging wood.

My antidepressants no longer work;

They don't understand the language of quarantine and isolation.

I commune with silent walls

with gritted teeth.

 I ramble more words

and I'm greeted with silence.

This boredom is driving me to the edge of my sanity.

Palliatives

Our palliatives have grown wings and

two legs –

Gone with the wind.

Hunger pangs sweep through the land like

a swarm of bees.

Our palliatives have been declared missing.

Hues and cries of the forgotten poor is

swirling like a whirlwind.

Our palliatives have been hoarded

by the ruling class.

It took more than timid limbs to wrestle our waylaid palliatives

from the heartless elites.

Not the End

Vaccines are not a signal of the end;

eradicate your ignorance that stinks like filthy rags.

The conspiracy theories flying are out of control;

these variants know no colour.

The numbers are rising like a gathering storm;

these revelations make the heart ache

in despair.

Trauma

Cold bodies, stiff –

The sight of mass graves drives me to the cliff.

Our trauma has no recess.

The statistics boggles the mind and

leaves a gaping void.

The song of remembrance is an unending tune.

Vaccine Wars

COVID wars are taking the place of
COVID jabs.
This cold war will have no victors.

European giants are engulfed in a muddy fight,
like pigs;
this mudslinging will not end well.

Survivors

The wall of remembrance holds up watertight memories –

of lives tossed by the whims and caprices of unstable men.

The paranoia of COVID sends us into a dark hole

and we sing an elegy as grief fouls the air.

Our lives are rocked like ships in a tumultuous storm,

My skin bears a testament – Pandemic Survivor.

One Good Man Short

The memories are not faint –

our larger-than-life father whose kindness spreads like river sand has crossed to the other side.

Father. Hero. Grandfather.

The epitome of love whose life shines brighter than a full moon.

Baba Nla, yours was a life lived in service to humanity.

The void you left and beautiful memories will never be forgotten.

A good man ascends to the celestial –

the earth lost a gem,

heaven gained an angel.

F*ck – F*cking 2020

How do we scrub 2020 from our history books?
How do we fuck it off
as a one-off?

The labels have left us weary,
pandemic torn and broken.
How do we deep-cleanse our minds
from the horrors of 2020?

The agony has left our mental health
shattered like splintered glass.

Do we lockdown the mind
or isolate it from further peril?

F*ck 2020

Rollback the years, fuck

twenty-twenty. Wipe out the

    scars that blurred that year.

Empty Rooms

My family house is a house of flying daggers,

of rivalries and bitter wars that eat deep, scarring every memory.

Some say blood is thicker than water.

Turn it on its head and say water is thicker than blood.

Last week, three strangers walked in through the back door.

Today, they hoisted our family's banner with pride.

COVAX

Some nations are crying wolf:

We can't afford the vaccines, they squeal,

Our people are dying in multitudes.

Their loud voices ring hollow.

These nations haunted by lack

only need to empty the account of some brazen looters

and they will be swimming

in the ocean of abundance.

One Jab

One jab

will reduce the death count.

One jab

will free us from lockdown.

One jab

will see us return to normalcy.

One jab

will wipe away our tears.

One jab

will end this evil narrative.

Grow Some Balls

My phone has been besieged by texts streaming in
like torrents of rain.
Lazy wankers flying the kite of COVID scams.

A pandemic amid a raging pandemic –
beware of unknown and non-existent parcels
and scam messages.

Before you click that link,
think.
Think twice!
Lest you're fleeced of your blood
and sweat.

Dream Farewell

Social distancing wrecked the dream farewell;

the third wave raged like a thunderstorm.

He spent his last days shielding and in isolation

and was buried in isolation.

His dream farewell was soured

with the hollow word: *Isolation.*

The Dead

The dead have buried their kind,

lest this pandemic take more prisoners in this raging inferno.

The living left us with no goodbyes

as they take a flight of no return.

There is a thin line between life and death;

it took a pandemic to unravel this truth.

Mask

Remove the mask.

Take off the covering that hides your identity.

Remove the mask.

Take off the veil of darkness that envelopes your shining light.

Remove the mask.

Remove the mask.

Remove the mask.

Home

Our home has become a den of fury

and rage.

When the busyness of life overshadowed it,

it was a nest of blooming love.

As the pandemic raged,

our love grew apart.

What is now left is the rubble of our once treasured love.

This Virus

This virus can't be wished away with rhetoric.

This virus can't be wiped away by hallucinations.

This virus can't be washed away from memory lane.

This virus has built a home on the sands of time.

Bewitched

My missus has been bewitched by fear;

our lips no longer lock together in passionate affection.

She is running away from an unseen virus;

her paranoia is infectious.

There are days I interlope with her fears rioting in my head.

I'm running scared from an invisible virus

that has turned our union into a loveless affair.

Thunderstorms

The figures of COVID-induced deaths in my postcode are frightening,

like a coming thunderstorm.

The rain of horror has swallowed valiant men and

the jaws of death have left sorrow pangs.

The sorrow of these COVID deaths cannot be washed by mere commiserations.

This numbing feeling eats deep into hearts.

Century Old

The century-old pandemic has reared its ugly head,

surging through nations like a conquering army facing no resistance.

The century-old pandemic has returned with calamity on its tail.

No one foresaw this looming calamity.

The eagle-eyed all went blind.

The second coming of the century-old pandemic has left sorrow

and ruin in its wake.

Dreams

The dreams were dark and lonely;

the dead were walking on a steep highway

before they disappeared into the night.

The ghost of my mother was humming a song in my left ear.

She says she needs a companion.

I'm losing my breath and the will to live on this lonely bed.

The dark nights pulled me away when my ventilator

would not give me one last dance.

Bankrupt

The bailiffs are at the front door.

I'm hiding away in the basement, enveloped by silence.

My wife says *I'm no longer a man.*

She says, *Real men don't hide.*

The after-effect of the pandemic is bankruptcy –

a pile of debt and scurrying away to the basement

when the bailiffs come calling.

Too Hot

Father says he is a prisoner.

Every day he wakes up swearing, breaking things,

blaming COVID.

Father says the house is too hot for comfort.

Every evening he stands in the hallway, cursing mother,

blaming COVID.

Father became a shadow

before he was lowered six feet underground.

My Remembrance

My remembrance of this pandemic will be to cry for the lives lost.

My remembrance of this pandemic will be to wrap in grief;

this grief can't be measured.

My remembrance of this pandemic will be layered in sorrow.

This cup of sorrow has left me on the brink.

My remembrance of this pandemic will be spent in isolation.

Stories

Paint the stories gory;

paint them red.

Paint the times cruel

and dark.

Paint the experience sorrowful

and nerve-wracking.

Paint this pandemic what it was –

a sordid misadventure.

The Days Are Running

The days are running into each other,
like turbulent waves overstretching their bank.

The nights are wild and long,
like an unending horror movie.

We move in and out of lockdowns,
like an airplane rocked by intermittent turbulence.

Our politicians say, *Oh shit,*
we are fucked; we have no clue.

I grew a few greys before we returned to normalcy.

Pandemic Times

This was a pandemic of the rich.

The rich became richer and fatter.

The poor got poorer and wallowed in the throes of poverty.

This was a battle of the rich against the poor.

The rich nations vaccinated and hoarded jabs.

The poorer nations were hit by brutal jabs to

the head and below the belt – scarring.

The pandemic times were denoted by the battle of the rich against the poor.

Frontline

It takes guts and selflessness to be on the frontline, fighting an invisible enemy with countless casualties.

The heroes were on the frontline, standing gallant.

It takes love and courage to go to war with an unseen enemy hoping for victory.

Fake News

I won't write an epistle on fake news.

The rumour mills fed us falsehood daily.

As the pandemic raged with fury,

fake news stung like a snake's fangs.

Born in Lockdown

The little one born in lockdown has grown a beard.

All his life has been spent in isolation.

He can't smell the flowers –

the sun cannot burn his skin.

Born in lockdown,

his life and times were denoted by lockdown.

The Great Apocalypse

I don't want to fall for the tripe of 5G and the great apocalypse.

Let me ignore that the world has come to a crushing end.

I read my Bible, skipping the Book of Revelation.

My unfulfilled dreams are keeping my hope alive.

I wish for continuity with all my heart –

No, this can't be the end.

Freedom Day

As Freedom Day inches nearer,

a new variant is wreaking havoc

in the neighbourhood.

This dream for normalcy remains an illusion.

As Freedom Day draws nigh,

scaremongering is peaking like an album topping the charts.

Will life ever be the same again?

As Freedom Day is around the corner,

the red light blinking is a sign there might be another wild goose chase.

COVID Survivor

Tattoo on my body in full caps:

COVID SURVIVOR.

I never tested positive for the virus,

but COVID infected me with panic attacks

and wild hallucinations.

This pandemic story can't be erased from our history books.

Our lives were clouded by loneliness,

chilling fear and untimely deaths.

We clapped and clapped for our NHS,

faces etched in delight as our clouds were covered with gloom.

Tears flowed like a river.

The pandemic knew no colours;

the whole world was united in grief.

Dreams

I have been dreaming all day.

I dreamt that COVID was a hoax,

an Oscar-winning movie

sold out in cinemas,

racking up streaming numbers on Netflix

and Amazon Prime.

I have been dreaming all day

that the last year never was.

I opened my dictionary and searched for the word *pandemic*;

it never existed.

I googled *Coronavirus*;

the page was missing.

I woke up panting, sweating, half-asleep.

I saw the news anchor reel out COVID death numbers in the last twenty-four hours.

My eyes widened to the painful reality.

Family

Strong family ties have been broken;

everyone feels like a distant relative.

The lockdown brought peril

and sowed disunity

in the family unit.

Passports

My international passport is out of date and gathering dust.

It is becoming a useless artefact.

My left arm carries so much weight

and immunity.

Domestic COVID

As isolation gathered steam

and lockdowns became a thing,

the malaise of abuse behind closed doors spiralled out of control.

Lovebirds before the virus hit home have become rivals;

some love nests turned to wrestling rings as the domestic virus ravaged homes.

Isolation and Lockdowns

Don't rewrite this as a one-off.

Never sugar-coat this with any feel-good vibes.

Evil winds blew with ferocious verve.

The world sunk to its knees

and a new low.

We wore the tag, homebound and shielding with no qualms.

History won't be turned on its head;

 it won't be re-written

or watered down.

Our lives were spent in isolation and lockdown.

Eat the Future Now

Tomorrow has been mortgaged by self-centred elites.

Yesterday, our stomachs rumbled in emptiness.

Today, we wore sullen faces in despair

as we found our hidden palliatives in secret warehouses.

Like an army of soldier ants,

we thronged and shared the crumbs that were rightfully ours.

Childhood

Childhood during the pandemic

was a summation of home-schooling and screaming parents.

In the living room, tempers flared every hour,

ruining a once-upon-a-time sacred love.

Childhood was denoted by boredom, isolation and weary faces;

emotions sweeping through the hallway were fever-pitch.

Childhood is a closed chapter forever.

Stay Home, Save Lives

This was an anthem for men with lesser power,

Stay home, save lives.

There was a recurring theme for the poor and weaklings,

Stay home, save lives.

We stayed at home until home became a magnetic force.

We stayed home to save lives,

not minding the elites who would not be restricted by the lockdown.

We found solace in our homes.

Through this action, many lives were saved.

Bio

Tolu' A. Akinyemi (also known as Tolutoludo & Lion of Newcastle) is a multi-award-winning Nigerian author in the genre of poetry, short story, children's literature and essays. His works include: *Dead Lions Don't Roar* (poetry, 2017), *Unravel Your Hidden Gems* (essays, 2018), *Dead Dogs Don't Bark* (poetry, 2018), *Dead Cats Don't Meow* (poetry, 2019), *Never Play Games with the Devil* (poetry, 2019), *Inferno of Silence* (short stories, 2020), *A Booktiful Love* (poetry, 2020), *Black ≠ Inferior* (poetry, 2021), *Never Marry a Writer* (poetry, 2021), *Everybody Don Kolomental* (poetry, 2021), *I Wear Self-Confidence Like a Second Skin* (children's literature, 2021), *I Am Not a Troublemaker* (children's literature, 2021), *Born in Lockdown* (poetry, forthcoming – September 2021), and *A god in a human body* (poetry, forthcoming – January 2022).

Tolu' has been endorsed by the Arts Council England as a writer with "exceptional talent". A former headline act at Great Northern Slam, Crossing the Tyne Festival, and Feltonbury Arts and Music Festival, he also inspires large audiences through spoken word performances. He has appeared as a keynote speaker in major forums and events and facilitates creative writing master classes to many audiences.

His poems have appeared in the 57th issue (Volume 15, no 1) of the *Wilderness House Literary Review*, *The Writers Cafe Magazine* Issue 18, GN Books, Lion and Lilac, and elsewhere.

His books are based on a deep reality and often reflect relationships and life and features people he has met in his journey as a writer. His books have inspired many people to improve their performance and/or their circumstances. Tolu' has taken his poetry to the stage, performing his written word at many events. Through his writing and these performances, he supports business leaders, other aspiring authors, and people of all ages interested in reading and writing. Sales of the books have allowed Tolu' to donate to charity, allowing him to make a difference where he feels it is important, and to show that he lives by the words he puts to the page.

He is a co-founder of Lion and Lilac, a UK-based arts organisation and sits on the board of many organisations.

Tolu' is a financial crime consultant as well as a Certified Anti-Money Laundering Specialist (CAMS) with extensive experience working with leading investment banks and consultancy firms.

He is a trained economist from Ekiti State University, formerly known as University of Ado-Ekiti (UNAD). He sat for his master's degree in Accounting and Financial

Management at the University of Hertfordshire, Hatfield, United Kingdom. Tolu' was a student ambassador at the University of Hertfordshire, Hatfield, representing the university in major forums and engaging with young people during various assignments.

Tolu' Akinyemi was born in Ado-Ekiti, Nigeria and lives in the United Kingdom. He is an ardent supporter of Chelsea Football Club in London.

You can connect with Tolu' on his various social media accounts:

Instagram: @ToluToludo

Facebook: facebook.com/toluaakinyemi

Twitter: @ToluAkinyemi

Author's Note

Thank you for the time you have taken to read this book. I hope you enjoyed the poems in it.

If you loved the book and have a minute to spare, I would appreciate a short review on the page or site where you bought it. I greatly appreciate your help in promoting my work. Reviews from readers like you make a huge difference in helping new readers choose a book.

Thank you!
Tolu' Akinyemi

Dead Lions Don't Roar

In a society where moral rectitude is increasingly becoming abeyant, Akinyemi's bounden duty is to reawaken it with verses. He, thus, functions as a philosopher-poet, a kind of factotum inculcating wisdom in different facets of life. *Dead Lions Don't Roar* leads us into the universe of an exact mind rousing the lethargic from indolence or prevarication, bearing in mind that the greatest achievers are those who take the bull by the horn. Taking a step can just be the open sesame to reach the stars. Enough of jeremiad! – **The Sun**

Dead Lions Don't Roar, a collection of poetic wisdom for the discerning, makes an interesting read. A paper pack, the poems are concise, easy to digest, travel friendly and express deep feelings and noble thoughts in beautiful and simple language. – **The Nation**

Akinyemi's verses are concise, straight-edge and explanatory, reminiscent of the kind of poetry often churned out by Mamman J. Vatsa, the late soldier and poet. – **yNaija**

Dead Lion's Don't Roar is a collection of inspiring and motivating modern-day verses. Addressing many issues close to home and also many taboo subjects, the poems reflect today's struggles and light the way to a positive future. This uplifting book will appeal to all age groups and anyone going through change, building or enjoying a career, or facing day-to-day struggles. Many of the short verses will resonate with readers, leaving them with a sense of peace and well-being.

Dead Dogs Don't Bark

Dead Dogs Don't Bark is as culturally relevant as can be, and this deserves commendation. – **Bellanaija**

In a nutshell, Dead Dogs Don't Bark is enjoyable, it is stimulating. - **Bdaily UK**

The collection takes this reader through an exhilarating journey of wits and pun. The power of words, both grand and subtle, is that it allows the reader to place himself in the scheme and feel the poems on a more visceral level.
Creating concrete imageries, the poet says even before it sticks out its tongue and bares its teeth, the first thing that defeats a fainthearted in an unfamiliar

threshold is the bark of a dog. It sends cold shivers running down the spine. That very bark, disarming as it is, is the dog's way of calling attention: I am here! - **Guardian Arts**

Dead Dogs Don't Bark is the second poetry collection from the acclaimed author Tolu' A. Akinyemi. With a similar tone and style to *Dead Lions Don't Roar* (Tolu's first poetry collection), this follow-up masterpiece is nothing short of pure motivation.

The poems cover a range of topics that many in life are aware of, that the author himself has experienced, and that we all, whatever our age, need support in. Beautifully written, the poems speak volumes to all age groups as they encourage finding your inner talent and celebrating your individuality and distinct voice.

The poetry collection contains didactic elements for negating the effects of peer pressure and criminality, along with many other forces. Also covering mental health, relationships, career focus, and general life issues, the poetry is, in turn, bittersweet, amusing and thought-provoking.

Dead Cats Don't Meow

In all, this poetry collection *Dead Cats Don't Meow* generally emphasizes the theme of self-belief and taking action. It reminds me of the saying "if you think you are too little to make an impact, try staying in a room with a mosquito." - **BellaNaija.**

Overall, *Dead Cats Don't Meow* comes across as a collection of thoughtful poetry that inspires, entertains, and educates its reader. It is a great blend of themes spanning across love, inspiration, politics, entrepreneurship, marriage and life, among others. Its simplicity eludes intentionality, and the plays on words show experience.

The collection is suitable for both the literary and non-literary community and is a great work for all manner of readers.

I believe, with this one, Akinyemi has achieved his goals of motivation.
- **The Nation Newspaper.**

Dead Cats Don't Meow urges its readers not to waste their ninth life... the author of this collection of poetic wisdom for the discerning adds his third compendium of poems to the bookshelves alongside *Dead Lions Don't Roar* and *Dead Dogs Don't Bark*. Tolu' A. Akinyemi, renowned poet, author and performer, brings to us *Dead Cats Don't Meow*, a metrical masterpiece which invokes love and respect for life with every word. Each poem examines a part of life, a sensation, a reaction, or an emotion. Beautifully written... individually, the verses breathe their own beat, whilst the collection knits together perfectly to present an idyllic collection to attain innate potential. Don't waste the ninth life! Don't miss the chance to add this rare compendium of poetic wisdom to your bookshelf today!

Unravel Your Hidden Gems

Unravel Your Hidden Gems is like a Solomon talking to us in the 21st century. The book teaches us to value what we have, the pursuit of excellence, and, above all, steps to unravel your hidden gems, drawn from your extraordinary talents, deposited in you right from the first day the placenta was severed from the womb. A book for all seasons, no doubt, especially in Africa where aspirations sometimes do not match inspirations, it is only logical that you add it to your shopping cart. - **Guardian Arts**

Watching others ascend the totem pole of life with relative ease, some come to believe they can't fly.

Times without number, they have tried, yet they have found no way to break the ice. Don't despair if you are unsettled by a losing streak.

Tolu Akinyemi, the author of *Unravel Your Hidden Gems,* believes that the hero lies in you. If only you can discover the hidden gems in you, you are on your way to excelling. How, then, do you dig deep into the labyrinth for the gems?

Unravel Your Hidden Gems is a 376-page book by a prolific UK-based Nigerian author. It is a collection of over 360 inspirational and motivational essays from a young man who feels he has a mission to rouse dampened spirits to make the much-needed push in life to regenerate abundantly.

In seven parts, the author makes a diligent search into typical problems encountered by men, capable of weighing them down, and comes up with snippets of wisdom. **- The Sun**

Unravel Your Hidden Gems is a collection of inspirational and motivational essays from the heart of the acclaimed author, Tolu' A. Akinyemi. Released hot on the heels of Tolu's first book of poetry, *Dead Lions Don't Roar*, this new book is a study on life, encouraging people to succeed at what they feel is important to their own happiness – be it their private life, business, religion, career, or relationships; each part of life is discovered. This mind-altering life manual can be read as a whole or visited in snippets for day-to-day inspiration. Each essay examines and highlights challenges in life and how to succeed in enjoying life with grace. A self-help study on life with a refreshing difference, the book is a totality of life's journey, reminding us we are here on a temporary basis and that it is our duty to not hide in obscurity, but to *Unravel Your Hidden Gems* before it is too late! Pure Inspiration!

Never Play Games with the Devil

TOLU' A. AKINYEMI

NEVER PLAY GAMES
WITH *The* DEVIL

Reflective, insightful, and ultimately inspirational, *Never Play Games with the Devil* is a collection best digested slowly and thoughtfully. It's a series of insights and admonitions about life's purposes and coping mechanisms for *"...not crashing under the weight of the world."*
D. Donovan, Senior Reviewer, Midwest Book Review

Readers will find Akinyemi's reflections on significant life issues completely relevant, sharply logical, and deeply felt. - **The Prairies Book Review**

Hear the poet as, in a succinct moment of self-adulation, he writes:

> *My brain thinks faster than my words can convey.*
> *My mind works magic. Can I live this life forever?*

Divided into three sections, *Never Play Games with the Devil* showcases a poet at the height of his powers, exploring several themes in different voices.

In the first section, the poet is the charismatic preacher encouraging people to hustle, find their feet and grow. He writes about the lot of broken men crashing under the weight of expectations; he talks about boys like Eddie and Edmund, bullied for the shape of their heads. He humorously addresses the consequence of choices in the title poem, *Never Play Games with the Devil*.

The second section secures him a seat as an activist. We see the poet tackle, in verse, despotic and undemocratic governments, marauding killer herdsmen, and the pastor who lost his voice. The poet mourns the hapless souls in the crossfire between society's rot and the State's insouciance.

The final poems explore the basis of human relationships. The poems here deal with love, commitment and trust.

Never Play Games with the Devil is a didactic collection of poems on pertinent life issues. These poems draw their appeal from the poet's ability to sustain a figment of thought through the entire span of each poem.

A Booktiful Love

Poet Tolu' A. Akinyemi tackles life with a passionate, analytical, observing eye and creates admonitions which pull at emotional strings in the heart. Poetry readers who choose his free verse collection will find it equally powerful whether it's considering divorce and grief or the love language of 'A Booktiful Love'. - **D. Donovan - Senior Reviewer, Midwest Book Review.**

Readers will find Akinyemi's collection an intriguing approach to exploration of the entirety of human experience in its various forms. This is a superb collection. - **The Prairies Book Review.**

A Booktiful Love is a collection of poems that deal with the entirety of human experience in its various forms. Didactically rich, the poems explore ideas ranging from love, relationships and patriotism to marriage, morality and many other concepts pertinent to daily living.

Given its variety of themes, what unifies the poems in this collection is the simplicity and ambiguousness of language that the poet employs. The poems draw their strength from their clarity and meaning.

These are poems with a purpose. Poet Tolu' A. Akinyemi doesn't shy away from this fact, as he writes in the poems *Writers* and *Write for Rights*. The poet's philosophy is evident in this collection. To him, a writer is saddled with the responsibility to use his words to teach, preach and fight for freedom.

He writes:

> *Let's change the world, one writer at a time,*
> *write those words till the world gets it right.*

Another special attribute to this collection is the poet's experimentation with words. This is clear right from the title. The poet identifies himself as a creator of words. The reader is obliged to travel into the mind of the writer in each poem, to understand how his mind works. As readers approach the end of this collection, they not only become engrossed in its didactic richness, but will also appreciate the uniqueness of the poet's style and the sense of responsibility he carries.

Inferno of Silence

Inferno of Silence is a wide-ranging collection that tackles different themes of love, life, interpersonal relationships, and social and political challenges. It's a hard-hitting, revealing collection that keeps readers engaged and thinking with each short exploration of characters who confront their prejudices, realities, and the winds of change in their lives.

Readers of literary explorations that include African cultural influence and modern-day dilemmas will find this collection engrossing. - **D. Donovan, Senior Reviewer, Midwest Book Review**

Poignant and honest...
Akinyemi's first collection of short stories dazzles with elegant prose, genuine emotions, and Nigerian cultural lore as it plumbs both the socio-cultural issues and the depths of love, loss, grief, and personal trauma. Lovers of literary fiction will be rewarded. - **The Prairies Book Review**

The first collection of short stories by this multitalented author entwines everyday events that are articulated in excellent storytelling.

The title story *Inferno of Silence* portrays men's societal challenges and the unspoken truths and burdens that men bear, while *Black Lives Matter* shows the firsthand trauma of a man facing racism as a footballer plying his trade in Europe.

Stories range from *Return Journey*, where we encounter a techpreneur/ poet/serial womanizer confronting consequences of his past actions, to *Blinded by Silence*, where a couple united by love must face a political upheaval changing their fortune.

These are completed with stories of relationships: *Trouble in Umudike* – about family wealth and marriage; *Everybody don Kolomental*, where the main character deals with mental health issues; and *In the Trap of Seers*, when one's life is on auto-reverse with the death of her confidante, her mother, as she takes us through her ordeal and journey to redemption. This is a broad and very inclusive collection.

BLACK ≠INFERIOR

Akinyemi employs a steady hand and heart to capturing Black lives in various nuances, from political and social arenas to personal experience: *"Equality is a forgotten child. The blood of the innocents/soil the World. Racial Injustice walks tall,/the graves of our ancestors quake in anguish/at this perpetual ignominy."*

This juxtaposition of the personal and the political makes *Black#Inferior* a particularly important read. It holds a compelling, accessible message to the Black community in the form of hard-hitting poems which offer emotional observations of the modern state of Black minds and societies around the world.

Poetry readers interested in the fusion of literary ability and social inspection will appreciate the hard-hitting blend of both in *Black#Inferior,* which is recommended reading for a wide audience, especially students of Black experience.- *D. Donovan - Senior Reviewer, Midwest Book Review.*

A celebration of black culture and experience and life in general, the collection makes for an electrifying read. - *The Prairies Book Review.*

Black ≠ Inferior is a collection of poems divided into 2 parts. The first part is a collection of thematically linked poems exploring Blackness and the myriads of issues it attracts. The second part oscillates themes— talking about consent, a query of death, a celebration of love among others. In his usual stylistic, this collection deals with weighty matters like race and colourism with simple and clear language.

In Black ≠ Inferior, we see Tolu' Akinyemi reacting in response to the world, to issues that affect Black people. Here, we see a poet shedding off his burdens through his poems; hence, the beauty of this collection is in the issues it attempts to address. In this collection, Tolu' wears a coat of many colours – he is a preacher, a prophet, a doctor and a teacher.

We see Tolu' the preacher in these lines:
'I wish you can rise through the squalor of poverty and voices that watercolour you as under-represented. I wish you can emblaze your name in gold, and swim against every wave of hate.'

This is a collection of poems fit for the present narrative as any (Black) person who reads this collection should beam with confidence at the end. This is what the poet sets out to achieve with his oeuvre.

NEVER MARRY A WRITER

Ultimately, the poet's caution to "Never Marry a Writer" is a deeper disclaimer, a warning that is more a promise. Writers, these poems remind the reader, bear witness. Whether evocative prose or colorful whimsy or the bleakest of forthright documentation, their words attest to the truths they observe. With its wily wordy ways, this collection reminds readers that even those without a literary spouse are nevertheless subject to--and on notice from--those who, like the author, observe and document. --- "The US Review of Books" (RECOMMENDED by the US Review)

"Bold, wry, and lyrical musings." -- *Kirkus Reviews*

OH, THE WEBS WE WEAVE...

For his seventh poetry collection, Tolu' has turned his attention to that old adage -
no one in a writer's life may have secrets.
A vibrant, human exploration of the way in which words and deeds connect all of us, and the tiniest movements which span out across continents.

Tolu' writes powerfully on family, love, loss, and with a scorching curiosity for the world around us. His readers will be familiar with his inimitable style, and this latest collection does not disappoint.

EVERYBODY DON KOLOMENTAL

At its core, the work is simply authentic and resonates both for its content and style. Delivering an almost lyrical sensation with the combination of smaller stanzas, the author's poetry references a multitude of life circumstances, including but not limited to middle school, therapy, and bachelorhood. Filled with poems that unveil a new gem of realization upon each subsequent reading, Akinyemi's poetry is a sure-fire must-read. --- "The US Review of Books". --- "The US Review of Books" (RECOMMENDED by the US Review)

A poignant collection that captures both the raw sorrows and joys of human existence.... --- "The Prairies Book Review"

Hope is Not Far Away…

Everybody Don Kolomental is a collection of poems that deal with everyday universal struggles.

Tolu' peddles hope to the lost and hopeless and pulls at the emotional strings of the heart in this collection of heartfelt poems. The collection mirrors life through the eyes of a deep-thinker and wordsmith.

Poet Tolu' A. Akinyemi knows the gravity of mental health struggles and uses his words as a soothing balm to heal readers of this collection.

In the poem titled 'Hope is not Far Away', he writes:

"Who will tell Okikiola that hope is not far away?

Its ship docked in the home of Akinyele before his candle was blown out and his flailing dreams were a shipwreck.

Who will tell Okikiola this is not the last straw?

These wind gusts would give way for the calming sea."

Whether you're in need of calm after the storm, therapy, healing, or to view everyday struggles from the lens of a veteran poet, this collection is for you.

A god IN A HUMAN BODY

Tolu' A. Akinyemi is a philosopher-poet and a deep thinker, and his journey into the realm of the spiritual would leave readers in awe.

A god in a human body is Tolu' A. Akinyemi's ninth poetry collection.

This collection is a meditation on the fleeting nature of human life. A god in a human body explores themes of spirituality, divinity and the enormous power that we possess while we traverse this earthly passage.

A god in a human body will take you on a rollercoaster of emotions and its pages will leave readers craving for more.

I AM NOT A TROUBLEMAKER

Chadwick has just joined a new school, and he is stung by the label of troublemaker.

Will the label stick, or will he get the chance to come clean?

I WEAR SELF-CONFIDENCE LIKE A SECOND SKIN

Matilda has been battling her fears at home and in school.

Will she be able to build her self-confidence or will she crumble under the weight of her fears?

www.ingramcontent.com/pod-product-compliance
Lightning Source LLC
Chambersburg PA
CBHW021447080526
44588CB00009B/728